# COLMA

*John Laue*

FUTURECYCLE PRESS

*Mineral Bluff, Georgia*

Published by FutureCycle Press
Mineral Bluff, Georgia, USA

ISBN 978-1-938853-16-6

# COLMA

## CITY OF THE DEAD /
### ELEGY FOR SKEPTICS

# COLMA

*(From the Spanish verb* colmar—*to fill to the brim,
to heap up, to overwhelm, to fulfill.)*

And the dark graves
multiply like footsteps.

# PREFACE

Colma is a town adjacent to San Francisco where most of the city's dead are buried. It has been called a necropolis because its population consists of hundreds of thousands dead in eighteen cemeteries for various nationalities and faiths. In this small village, the dead outnumber live residents by more than a thousand to one.

While in graduate school at San Francisco State University, I got a job in Colma. The large Greek family I worked for owned a plant nursery, flower shop, and mortuary. My job consisted mostly of delivering bouquets and elaborate arrangements called flower pieces to cemeteries, mortuaries, and other places for funerals. Sometimes I arrived while ceremonies were still going on; at other times, I had to search out the proper tombstones among many rows and sections of giant cemeteries to place bouquets in receptacles attached to them. This job got me through a year and a half of grad school.

I grew to love the town of Colma. Some of the cemeteries were like large, peaceful sculpture gardens. Occasionally, long after I stopped working for the Pappas family, I'd go there on a sunny day and bask in the beauty and tranquility. Colma features an abundance of angels and other religious symbols, but what I really loved were the numerous varieties of trees and flowers in an atmosphere of extreme peace. I lost most of my fear of death there and was so inspired that I wrote my impressions as poetry. The two sections of this book — *City of the Dead* and *Elegy for Skeptics* — are the result.

—J. L.

# CITY OF THE DEAD

*There is no greater impetus to action*
*than the thought of death.*

# CONTENTS

# PROLOGUE

Like an iceberg the city of death
leans into the shadows of late afternoon,
leans and wanes in the sunset,
only its crown exposed.

Now to its alleys, terraces,
groves of sighing trees,
curved roads, lonely shrines,
windowless monuments to great names,
silence of the night arrives.

Gone are voices of the living
who move in circles here
like woodsmen who have lost their compasses;
gone the low insistence of motors
as one group of mourners, then another,
went among stone-studded rows,
depositing flowers.

In bright moonlight
geometry of marble echoes, re-echoes.
Here one could almost see
not cemeteries, but a city of crystal,
core of a growing city which,
like coral,
we build for more than just ourselves.

# —I—
# THE WISH

I pose a question for you now, necropolis,
city of raised pedestals, spread crosses,
miles of artifacts, transitory passages.

All this layered land
seems rife with vital messages.
Are there beginnings here for me
where meanings intersect
with paths of mute finality?

I have prepared my mind
to sift your landscapes,
winnow your terrain.

My plan: to probe massed monuments,
commune with stone-walled tombs,
explore your breeze-blown flower farms,
your leaf-quiet groves
perhaps to better know myself.

Let me unwind your silences,
your vaunted confidentiality,
find if the peace you advertise can thrive
in an awakened, questing brain.

# —II—
# A COMMENT

For miles on every side great portals stand,
each with its proper name, its shaded lawns,
its granite memories.

Here are *The Fields of Peace,*
bold signs announce.  Here is *The Wishing Well.*
And black processions bear their burdens
in and out, disgorging corpses, coins, flowers.

The world of the dead is quiet, orderly,
kept by custodians of intricate geometry,
its loudest sound the subtle swish of money.

# —III—
# THE FEAR

Colma, city of many alleyways and passages
where the living trace their patterns
periodically:

> Up hill, down hill,
> turn and circle
> in perpetual search.

> Step gingerly, my friend;
> some of this dirt is soft and wet,
> may suck your feet,
> sink you into your mother's arms.

I fear your set finality, dead city:
you are where man's scent gives out,
where trails of money end,
where intricate, twisted threads of lives
converge in a huge, inescapable net.

# —IV—
## FLOWERS AND COFFINS

Colma, city of flowers and coffins,
where grass stirs in western breezes,
winks in winter showers.

Blossoms weep from stem-ends
at the funerals of the rich,
and even the poor lie tended.

Gardeners move with hoses
among rows of groping plants,
send out watery hosannas.

Periodically blooms emerge:
live sentences of color hang in air,
follow sun in crowded fields.

Bouquets beautify brief funerals,
end their short-lived cycles
in great compost piles.

Here is momentary grace: a ceremony
while, in the next bright scape,
live blossoms dance:

thin stems flutter in the wind;
round crowns bob like small umbrellas;
all heads bow in unison.

# —V—
## LOVERS AND HONEYBEES

Colma, land of laid and fallow lovers,
some with lusty drops remaining,
and a billion tiny rootlets
reaching blindly for a taste of moisture;

land where each caressing wind
sends its vibrations underground
along a million flowers' dancing stems
to where corpses lie with dirt-clods in their mouths;

nature's land, where in their proper seasons
come the honey gatherers
to enter every hollow blossom,
fertilizing, scraping, pollinating.

Colma, city of blooms, dead lovers, bees
all with their cycles intertwining.

O people of discriminate tastes,
when you sit in San Francisco
over breakfast honeycombs,
will you turn your minds to these?

# —VI—
## A FUNERAL

From the hill, a slow procession
moves like a stream of glossy beetles
single file among patterns
close-set graveplots make.

Now they wind
up the long circular drive.

The lead car stops,
its black length catching the sun.
1874-1965.

Another cycle is completed.
We cling to the numbers and are comforted:
this is how we try to make an order.

Perhaps in ten thousand years
archeologists will wonder,
as we might about the Mayans,
was there ever anything here
but monuments and numbers?

# —VII—
# THE MILITARY CEMETERY

A field of close-trimmed green
with rows of cold white stones
immaculate as dominoes
set straight at regulation distances.

The graves march up a rolling hill,
then lap over, vanishing below the crest
as if they might go on forever.

Soldiers, sailors, airmen, marines—
their ranks all equal now,
they lie in strict formation
under these extreme conditions.

As wars repeat,
entrenched battalions of the dead
forever hold their dark positions.

# —VIII—
## THE GREEK CEMETERY

At the Greek cemetery, people chant a prayer
while bees rise in a stunning spiral flight.
Mourners raise their heads to watch
the swarmers humming.

There are no angels here that fly like bees,
or chase a queen, or fall from air.
Their massive wings outspread,
blank-eyed seraphim stare straight ahead
as the low hum dies away.

The people stand transfixed,
their minds still upward.
A great hush settles on the land.

O world of textures, sounds, sights,
entrancing landscapes, lovely Colma,
are you held in these stone angels' hands?

# —IX—
# THE ITALIAN CEMETERY

No simple crosses here,
but every size and shape of marble,
crowding out the grass,
spreading to the edges
of the pointed iron gates.

Here in the Italian plots
the dead seem richer than the living,
each with elaborate carving,
mute, stone-sculptured grace.

There is little path to walk upon:
this blocking caters to still feet;
final gestures of insurance
expensive, geometric monuments
which stand like fortresses,
separate touched life from death.

Only the very poor
dwell in the clotted ground.
The rest shrink slowly with great elegance
like the final scions of a noble family
caring only that the name survives,
is not dishonored as it burns
into their foreheads' wizen lines.

# —X—
# GARDENERS

Down row on row impassive gardeners walk
among monuments or in flower farms,
bending then straightening,
hoeing, raking, cutting ragged grass,
cupping with warm hands the fragile plants.

Rank steam rises from wet ground;
cloud banks roll like waterwheels.
Water into earth, from earth to sky again;
the cycle turns with time,
while around its girth speed other cycles
as the spiral galaxy revolves,
flies eternally apart.

Dirt-gloved gardeners walk alone,
or stroll in twos and threes,
intent but never hurrying,
these solemn nurses of the universe.
All have the look, if not the absolute ease,
of men with peaceful hearts.

# —XI—
## TENTATIVE ENDING

O inverted city,
city of strange, bitter fluids,
of shadowy arches, stone projections,
city with foundations of damp bone,
how your peace attracts me.

Silent gardeners move among the tombs.
Shall I apply? Shall I stay here permanently,
curry the landscape of the dead,
carry the soil from grave or flowerbed,
lovingly cut the grass in a geometry of shadows?

The summer rain beats messages
like drum-rolls to my taut imaginings.
Dead hands stretch upward towards me,
some with a sign of peace
made by their shrinking fingers.

Worms hear the pelting of rain and rise.
Night-crawlers almost as long as penises
expand, contract, stretch under rains,
their blind ends conscious
of the ground's moist sweetness.

O the coolness of wet sidewalks,
slippery, voluptuous grass.
Better this than poisonous fluid
puddled in those tangled veins.

Worms stretch, contract,
work their single immaculate muscle.

Below them, stiff dead wait for their assault
which must come sometime
if our bodies are to take their part
in greater cycles when our lives are done.

Soon the rain will stop, moisture rise;
visible steam will float up from the ground
as hot sun sucks, fresh winds blow.
Even planets, solar systems, galaxies
will live through massive cycles.

But now a voice inside me says,
*Forget the fallow dead.*
*You have another life to live,*
*a little movement bolstered by your bones.*
*One small cycle, but it is your own.*

# —XII—
# THE OPENING

Open the huge, intricate gates,
set up picnic tables;
invite the people of the city in.

Let the old Chinese come here
to play tight games of mah-jong.
Set up some courts for bocce ball.
Let the Greeks dance, the Irish sing.

Let lovers come, linger in these quiet groves,
kiss, stroke each other's thighs.

Let businessmen from concrete depths
set up their offices with leafy walls,
informally conduct each day's appointments.

Let them all come here
who strive in paltry parks
for space to set a picnic cloth;
who wander through museums, lonely, full of sadness;
whose every moment is composed
of concrete, asphalt, metal, paper, plastic.

Those who are giving up on life,
let them come in,
sit on the grass whose chemicals contain
the essence of their ancestors,
eat sandwiches, have therapy
among the blooms of flower eyes.

Colma, your beauty is not for the dead,
not even in war,
when they multiply more swiftly than the living.

# —XIII—

# THE MAD DANCE

Let these grounds be freed of fear
whose feet on tiptoe never touch the grass.

Let eyes that strain in sideways fright
at claw-like shadows of twigs
or sudden sibilant sounds be opened.

Dance till the graves themselves fall open
with a great suck of wind,
show their bland, disintegrating contents:

      Stumps rot in the mind
      while moony water leeches them.
      We turn around three times, and lo,
      our warts are gone; our warts,
      multiplying lives imagined
      full of cancer, cells gone crazy,
      paralyzing, even killing—

Let the graves of our minds open up to the sun,
expose their superstitious fillings!

# —XIV—

# THE APOLOGY

O Mother Grave, forgive me:
I have not kept your silence.

I have swung in the light of love
through hollow groves
where tentacles of willows
swept away the sound;

I have stood on one foot,
balanced on deep, chiseled letters,
fell, stamped messages
on new-turned ground.

I have dropped a corner
of the casket singing,
hung the flower piece
around a horse's neck.

O I have spread your shadowy fields
with rank manure, Mother Grave.
Now what can I expect?

*No more or less than all my little ones:*
*a chilly hole no bigger than your bones.*
*But someday when all critical eyes are gone,*
*I'll fill your skull with crystal for this song.*

# —XV—
## ONE LAST LOOK

How dazzling when, at dawn,
under red and rolling clouds,
the cemeteries stand
thick-glazed with light,
dew still on the grass,
the long sun shining.

Hands that will never hold
the colors of dawn
tighten into fists,
their tendons drying rawhide;
feet curl in darkness;
lungs grow leathery as punching bags.

The relatives we touched,
kissed, fought,
all lie here quietly
shrinking into nothingness.

It is so difficult to say
there is an end:
no more lusty loins,
happy thoughts or angers;
only the dark unfeeling dissolution.

Underneath each grassy mound
water gropes for union,
universal solvent
processing the essences of man.

No casket can withstand
its entrances forever.

Our rich flesh will end
as innocent solutions
seeping downward
far beneath the living lushness
of the surface.

We shall be free chemicals,
remains of cancelled lives,
separate elements
in dark, obscure,
but ever-flowing springs
and underground rivers.

# EPILOGUE

Goodbye Colma, dark, bright,
city of sealed monuments, soaring trees,
assembled angels, firm, unbroken natural laws.

From your unceasing cycles
I have gleaned a rule of energy:
endings do engender green beginnings.

I will mourn no more
for your disintegrating corpses,
nor be your faithful messenger
between the living and the dead.

Years with you are now rich memories
of mute fertility where death reverts to nature,
deep-sunk coffins watered by warm tears.

O city of eternal changes,
verdant fields, industrious bees,
I leave your grounds with newfound peace,
a clearer voice, relief from cares;
leave with you these well-discarded remnants,
stem-ends of a hundred youthful fears.

# ELEGY FOR SKEPTICS

*In most important matters
the price of certainty is blindness.*

# CONTENTS

—I—
# THE PASSING

*(For Lennie Lasher)*

Did death break like a wave
over his pillowed head?
Or did it come in tiny increments,
soft steps upon a stair?
They'd no way of knowing,
standing there like butlers
waiting for assignments.

He was dead and they were caught
in the midst of reveries,
amazed.

They'd expected a rattle
to come bubbling from his chest,
or lacking that, even the slightest tremor
signaling the end would have sufficed.

But there was nothing visible.
Only under the sealed and fevered lids
a certain little light slid from his eyes
and Harry left them poised above an empty space.

They leaned like parentheses
over the peaceful face.
Each wanted to speak
but there were no words,
only the sound of wind beating the curtains
over the windowsill.

# THE EMBALMER

At the town's tail end
Phil, the little embalmer,
hums a dirge-like ditty:
song of all the sharp things,
the coverings, the consummations,
the gentle and maniac violences,
the entrances, the exits,
the self-contained decays,
the local and general injuries,
the breakages and desecrations;
he's seen them all.

He sings of the precision of the carpenter:
Harry's casket is a masterpiece
of mortise and tenon accuracy,
its lid designed to fit the shadow perfectly.
Phil sings that everything is in its place
and, singing, he enjoys his art,
turns the body to a shell,
replaces all life's fluids with bitter wine.

We may envy him
for he sees meaning here:
death is his life.
Under a day-bright neon light
his quick hands flicker in and out
with practiced grace;
his taxidermy shows the stroke of genius.

He's grown calm
since he came to his trade,
saw the blind and final shape
of each man's fate
spread out before him on the table.

# —III—
# THE CLERGY

Reverend Ric, a local minister, declares
we'll have *La Vie Eternelle*:

*It's God's will that for each there's a time*
*when life meets death:*
*the organs hang like cities*
*in the belly of the night*
*and wink out one by one,*
*the trains of the blood grow silent;*
*death hunkers on the cooling tracks.*
*But the soul! —The soul does rise*
*like a newly loosed balloon.*

Perhaps we should have faith,
but darkness shuffles overhead
confusing as a pack of cards
in a black magician's hands
and we begin our questioning again.

Is it a god that comes impersonally
in the shape of planes,
or clouds, or horses set like
random dominoes inside a fence?

Or clothed as a man, red-bearded?
brown-skinned? blue-eyed?
Or as a woman,
in the sag of her breasts?
in the curl at her thighs?

Shadows thick as blankets dim our eyes,
engender discontent.

Is it to a god, the dead, or death itself
that we dedicate these monuments?

# —IV—
## THE MASON

*Some of our greatest art*
*is in remembrance of the dead,*
remarks Fred O., the mason.
*Think of the pyramids.*
*See where the planes of tombs*
*and mausoleums meet the wind*
*and gesture man's magnificence.*

These monuments to human greatness stand
like silent, massive ships,
all sealed, all keeping in the darkness.

Yet at dawn, the tents of shadow stay
as definite as all our stone facades.
And in the afternoon, the shadows stretch
across the landscape, lengthening
till evening comes and leaves us small
and cautious in our blindness.

What frightened lines we sometimes speak,
thinking of man's magnificence
while huddled in our rooms,
eyes full of fearsome images,
hearts rattled by the wind—
we—the chosen people of the darkness.

# —V—
# THE PHILOSOPHER

Art B., a philosopher of my acquaintance,
expounds on death:

*we can't insult the figures in the coffins:*
*they've been carefully cared for,*
*rinsed out, purged, and pickled*
*till they're little more than simulacrums*
*of living flesh.*

*The owners of the bodies wouldn't care*
*if we drew and quartered them,*
*pried their tendons from their bones,*
*stuck needles in their drying eyes.*

It's for themselves
the preachers' fingers waggle by the grave,
the masons chisel cunning corners on the stones,
the carpenters grip the coffin nails
as if they were alive.

It's for themselves
the poets, long-faced in dim lamplight,
write of death.

Each provides their own distractions,
sends up small balloons of metaphor.

But the ball of shadow
in the corpse's open mouth
speaks louder.

# —VI—

# THE MUSICIAN

*For my funeral,* ventures Lennie,
my musician friend,
(an aging virtuoso),
*play a booming exorcism.*

*Let the drums rumble syncopated rhythms*
*and the flutes insinuate*
*above the innuendos of the clarinets.*
*Let the brass blare its whorish blare*
*and stare at the crowd with multiple eyes,*
*and give the triangle to a minister*
*to play three-cornered notes.*
*Might that be enough to wake the dead?*

But even if our ancient mummies rose
in choirs of hallelujah,
winding bandages around a maypole,
or singing praise to science,
would it matter much
except to make an over-populated world?

Some would sermonize about it,
some hoist glasses at loud cocktail parties,
some play fateful games of chance.

But each would hear his own internal voices,
each his body's rhythms, slowing, speeding,

each his heart, his vulnerable heart,
which may hesitate in death's presence,
then race out like hoofbeats
of a startled deer.

# —VIII—
# A FRIEND

After solemn words of remembrance,
Harry's body sinks below. The mourners leave
but Paul A., closer to him,
lingers by the grave.

For a dream-like hour he meditates
as shadows lengthen
and assert their evening dominance:

*Is it this we live for, only this —*
*a continuity of generations dead?*
*a civilization founded on our bones?*

*Then what is life but singing for the dead?*
*We whistle in the dark*
*and all our art and industry*
*amount to nothing but a hill of stones.*

*Yet when we've stood half-hypnotized*
*before the grave's grim depths*
*there's much we must express.*
*Can we find a melody and keep to it?*

*I've seen people sing with all their might,*
*religiously, and nothing came of it.*
*They spend their lives as I do mine,*
*assailed by fears and doubts.*

*That's what we have in common, I suppose:*
*most of us feel small*
*when faced with death's stern law,*
*more inclined to whisper than to shout.*

*Yet perhaps we could sing with some assurance*
*that with or without glib promises of heaven,*
*we all become as children*
*under the eyelids of our nights;*

*that we now can reach past far horizons*
*letting our sweet and bitter anthems flow,*
*as everywhere, with swift, consistent rhythms*
*dark precisely balances light.*

# ACKNOWLEDGMENTS

This book was originally published as a chapbook by the same name by FutureCycle Press in 2008. This edition has expanded content and photographs not included in the original work.

-

*Photographs by John Laue; author photo by Jennifer Lagier; cover design, photo treatments, and interior book design by Diane Kistner (dkistner@futurecycle.org); Book Antiqua text with Anklepants titling*

# ABOUT FUTURECYCLE PRESS

FutureCycle Press is dedicated to publishing lasting English-language poetry and flash fiction books, chapbooks, and anthologies in both print-on-demand and ebook formats. Founded in 2007 by long-time independent editor/publishers and partners Diane Kistner and Robert S. King, the press incorporated as a nonprofit in 2012. A number of our editors are distinguished poets and authors in their own right, and we have been actively involved in the small press movement going back to the early seventies.

The FutureCycle Poetry Book Prize and honorarium is awarded annually for the best full-length volume of poetry we publish in a calendar year. Introduced in 2013, our Good Works projects are devoted to issues of global significance, with all proceeds donated to a related worthy cause. We are dedicated to giving all authors we publish the care their work deserves, making our catalog of titles the most distinguished it can be, and paying forward any earnings to fund more great books.

We've learned a few things about independent publishing over the years. We've also evolved a unique, resilient publishing model that allows us to focus mainly on vetting and preserving for posterity the most books of exceptional quality without becoming overwhelmed with bookkeeping and mailing, fund-raising activities, or taxing editorial and production "bubbles." To find out more about what we are doing, come see us at www.futurecycle.org.

www.ingramcontent.com/pod-product-compliance
Lightning Source LLC
LaVergne TN
LVHW051802080426
835511LV00018B/3386